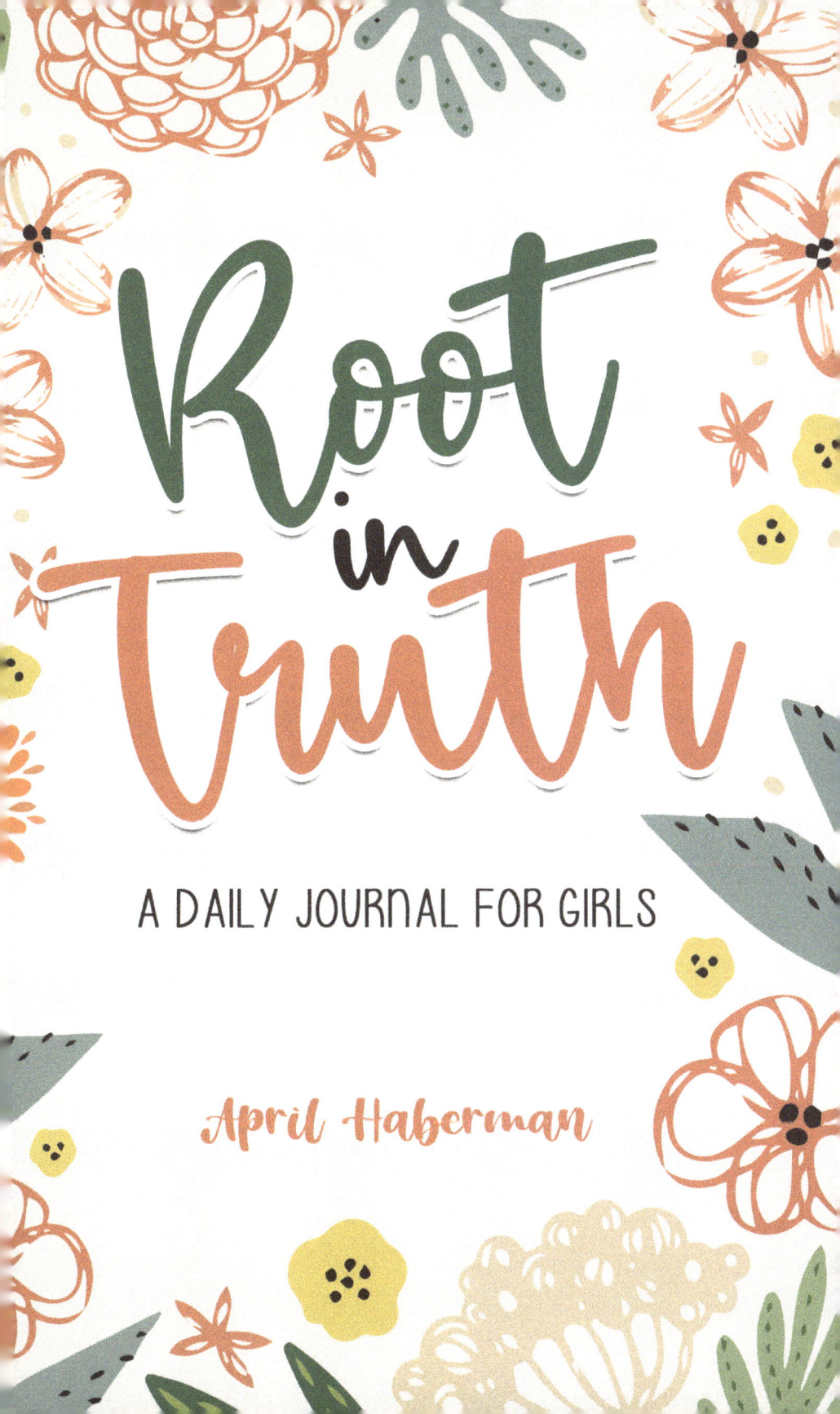

Root in Truth

A DAILY JOURNAL FOR GIRLS

April Haberman

To my most favorite girl in the world- Rachael. Your confidence, compassion, and love are my inspiration. I love you. Mom

Contents

Author's Thoughts

Welcome! I know that journaling can be life-changing. And, I also know that it's not easy to stare at a blank piece of paper. What do you write and where do you start?

This journal is designed to get you started, to deepen your relationship with God, and to get your pen moving across the page. Journaling is for YOU. It's a place for you to share your feelings, explore your dreams and to spend time being a bit creative. Journaling gives you space to spend time with yourself and with God.

I pray that this will inspire you to celebrate the woman you are becoming by spending time each day recognizing your feelings, drawing and doodling, and coloring outside the lines. Be your beautiful YOU!

May you find JOY in the journey, girls!

Questions

We've all been there. Staring at blank journal pages with a desire to start, but not quite sure what to write. I suggest picking one or two of the questions below and grabbing a pen to begin. I promise, once your journal isn't blank anymore, it feels more natural to write. Go ahead, get something on your paper!

- What's happening in my life today, tomorrow, this week?
- What help do I need from God?
- What questions do I have for God?
- What scripture speaks to me when I think about what's happening in my life or what I need from God?
- Can't make a decision? Ask God for wisdom and direction.

Put it into practice

Take a few minutes and give it a try!

Feelings

We often write or make lists and rarely notice how we feel. That means we stay in our heads (or thoughts) most of the time and don't connect to the heart. Be sure to connect with your feelings. Ask yourself:

How does this make me feel?
What emotions bubble up?

Having trouble naming that feeling? Here's a list:

- Happy
- Vibrant
- Confused
- Anxious
- Ashamed
- Joyful
- Blessed
- Blah
- Relaxed

- Ignored
- Sad
- Angry
- Inspired
- Upset
- Calm
- Peaceful
- Frustrated
- Weary

- Doubtful
- Jealous
- Drained
- Puzzled
- Strong
- Depressed
- Afraid

Put it into practice

Take a few minutes and give it a try! Look at what you wrote on the previous page and write down how it makes you feel.

Gratitude

Gratitude keeps your eyes looking UP!

As you journal, you may want to include a few things you are grateful for each day. It's hard to have a bad day when we remind ourselves of our blessings. One of our greatest gifts from God is choice. *We can choose what to focus on.* By choosing to count our blessings, we are choosing to keep our eyes looking up! *Psalm 118:24*

Remember, when you journal you're talking to God. He's not concerned with how you say things. No need to be fancy. God just wants your heart. So, share it freely!

Put it into practice

Take a few minutes and give it a try! Things I'm grateful for today:

-
-
-

-
-
-

Joy List

What fills you with joy? Start a list you can go back to over and over again, especially on days you don't feel great about yourself or life just has you feeling down. You can always go to your joy list and fill your soul- it's a good pick me up! *Isaiah 55:12*

1.

2.

3.

4.

5.

6.

7.

8.

Dreams

What are your hopes & dreams? Tell God about them. Ask Him to inspire and to lead you. Want to take it one step further? Create a dream board. There are a ton of free how-to resources online and at the library for your reference. Write out a few of your dreams below (or paste pictures and words from magazines). *Jeremiah 29:11*

Scripture Search

Want to dive into Scripture? Try Scripture search for a few weeks. Write down what's happening in your life or questions or prayers you have for God, and then write a Scripture reference that inspires you or helps you to hear God's voice. Don't know where to find that perfect Scripture reference? Try using your Index to Scriptures, Index to Notes, and Concordance in the back of your Bible. Color code your three categories/ questions so it's easy to look back on and see how God has been working in your life. I like using pink, purple, and green pens… but just pick your favorites! *Psalm 46:10*

What's happening in my life?

Questions or prayers I have for God:

Scripture reference:

Color & Doodle

Do you like to color? Sometimes it's easy to draw and doodle instead of writing. Color can always brighten your day. Pick a word from the Bible that inspires you. Write it down, color, or doodle it! You can color outside the lines and have fun with this. After all, it's YOUR journal and it's about YOUR uniqueness. Be YOU! *Psalm 139:13*

Reflection

Journaling at night can feel better for some people. Good news! This is a really healthy habit. Reflecting on the day allows us to examine our actions & feelings and gives us quiet time to pray. Try reflecting on the following topics or questions:

How did God provide for me today?

How did I see God at work?

What am I grateful for?

How did I feel today?

What drew me closer to God today and what pulled me away? What can I learn from this?

Prayer:

I AM Affirmations

Trustworthy
Important Accepted Necessary
Ambassador of Christ Known by God
Forgiven Holy
Bought by a Price
Adopted into God's Family Guided & Led
Strengthened by Him Adopted into God's Family Entrusted
Entrusted Strengthened by Him Holy
Protected A Child of God Significant
Blessed A Work of Art Significant Light of the World
Blessed A Saint A Work of Art Beloved
Beloved Trustworthy Spiritually Alive
Blameless Cared For Set Apart
Righteous Ambassador of Christ Set Apart A New Creation
Righteous Temple of God
A Masterpiece Chosen A Child of God
Redeemed
Light of the World Made in God's Image Temple of God
God's Messenger Forgiven Blameless Made in God's Image
Necessary God's Messenger
Bought by a Price Appointed
A Citizen of Heaven A New Creation Salt of the Earth
Worthy Loved A Friend
Made Strong A Saint Fearfully & Wonderfully Made
Guided & Led
Delivered
Justified

Whole & Complete Redeemed
Cared For Spiritually Alive Blessed
A Masterpiece Justified
Loved Delivered
Accepted Whole & Complete Very Good
Very Good
A Citizen of Heaven
A Royal Priesthood Important A Friend
A Child of God
Chosen Worthy
A Royal Priesthood
Righteous Set Free
Very Good
Made Strong
Salt of the Earth Protected
Set Free
Righteous
Appointed

I AM
Set Apart
Very Good
Chosen
A Masterpiece

www.Good2BGirl.com

Thank You

I hope you create a daily habit of talking to God, writing in your journal, and expressing yourself. You've had time to practice. How does it make you feel to connect to God and get in tune with your true self? I hope you've gained confidence in your journaling!

Don't stop here just because you've completed your practice section. Keep going! The more you practice, the easier journaling becomes. You'll find your own rhythm and favorite way to journal. I encourage you to go back through this journal when you're done to see how you've grown spiritually.

Stay rooted in Him, my sister in Christ. May you grow and bloom. YOU are pretty awesome!

Ephesians 2:10

April

Date:

What am I grateful for today?

-
-
-

-
-
-

Questions & Reflection:

Scripture:

Daily Affirmation: I AM…

Color, Doodle & Notes

Be your beautiful YOU!

Date:

What am I grateful for today?

-
-
-

-
-
-

Questions & Reflection:

Scripture:

Daily Affirmation: I AM...

Be your beautiful YOU!

Date:

What am I grateful for today?

-
-
-

-
-
-

Questions & Reflection:

Scripture:

Daily Affirmation: I AM...

Be your beautiful YOU!

Date:

What am I grateful for today?

-
-
-

-
-
-

Questions & Reflection:

Scripture:

Daily Affirmation: I AM...

Be your beautiful YOU!

Date:

What am I grateful for today?

-
-
-

-
-
-

Questions & Reflection:

Scripture:

Daily Affirmation: I AM...

Be your beautiful YOU!

Date:

What am I grateful for today?

-
-
-

-
-
-

Questions & Reflection:

Scripture:

Daily Affirmation: I AM...

Be your beautiful YOU!

Date:

What am I grateful for today?

-
-
-

-
-
-

Questions & Reflection:

Scripture:

Daily Affirmation: I AM...

Be your beautiful YOU!

Date:

What am I grateful for today?

-
-
-
-
-
-

Questions & Reflection:

Scripture:

Daily Affirmation: I AM...

Be your beautiful YOU!

Date:

What am I grateful for today?

-
-
-

-
-
-

Questions & Reflection:

Scripture:

Daily Affirmation: I AM...

Be your beautiful YOU!

Date:

What am I grateful for today?

-
-
-

-
-
-

Questions & Reflection:

Scripture:

Daily Affirmation: I AM...

Be your beautiful YOU!

Date:

What am I grateful for today?

-
-

-
-

-
-

Questions & Reflection:

Scripture:

Daily Affirmation: I AM...

Be your beautiful YOU!

Date:

What am I grateful for today?

-
-
-
-
-
-

Questions & Reflection:

Scripture:

Daily Affirmation: I AM...

Be your beautiful YOU!

Date:

What am I grateful for today?

-
-
-

-
-
-

Questions & Reflection:

Scripture:

Daily Affirmation: I AM...

Be your beautiful YOU!

Date:

-
-
-

-
-
-

Questions & Reflection:

Scripture:

Daily Affirmation: I AM...

You
Are
Loved

For God so loved the world that he gave his one and only Son, that whoever believes in him shall not perish but have eternal life.

———————————

John 3:16 (NIV)

How does it make you feel to know this?

Date:

-
-
-

-
-
-

Be your beautiful YOU!

Date:

What am I grateful for today?

-
-
-

-
-
-

Questions & Reflection:

Scripture:

Daily Affirmation: I AM…

Be your beautiful YOU!

Date:

What am I grateful for today?

-
-
-

-
-
-

Questions & Reflection:

Scripture:

Daily Affirmation: I AM...

Be your beautiful YOU!

Date:

What am I grateful for today?

-
-
-
-
-
-

Questions & Reflection:

Scripture:

Daily Affirmation: I AM...

Be your beautiful YOU!

Date:

What am I grateful for today?

-
-
-

-
-
-

Questions & Reflection:

Scripture:

Daily Affirmation: I AM...

Be your beautiful YOU!

Date:

What am I grateful for today?

-
-
-

-
-
-

Questions & Reflection:

Scripture:

Daily Affirmation: I AM...

Be your beautiful YOU!

Date:

What am I grateful for today?

-
-
-

-
-
-

Questions & Reflection:

Scripture:

Daily Affirmation: I AM...

Be your beautiful YOU!

Date:

What am I grateful for today?

-
-
-
-
-
-

Questions & Reflection:

Scripture:

Daily Affirmation: I AM...

Be your beautiful YOU!

Date:

-
-
-

-
-
-

Questions & Reflection:

Scripture:

Daily Affirmation: I AM...

Be your beautiful YOU!

Date:

What am I grateful for today?

-
-
-

-
-
-

Questions & Reflection:

Scripture:

Daily Affirmation: I AM...

Be your beautiful YOU!

Date:

-
-
-

-
-
-

Questions & Reflection:

Scripture:

Daily Affirmation: I AM...

Be your beautiful YOU!

Date:

What am I grateful for today?

-
-
-

-
-
-

Questions & Reflection:

Scripture:

Daily Affirmation: I AM...

Date:

What am I grateful for today?

-
-
-
-
-
-

Questions & Reflection:

Scripture:

Daily Affirmation: I AM...

Be your beautiful YOU!

Date:

What am I grateful for today?

-
-
-

-
-
-

Questions & Reflection:

Scripture:

Daily Affirmation: I AM...

Color, Doodle & Notes

Be your beautiful YOU!

You
Are
Worthy

But God showed His love to us. While we were still sinners, Christ died for us.

———————————

Romans 5:8 (NIV)

How does it make you feel to know this?

Date:

What am I grateful for today?

-
-
-

-
-
-

Questions & Reflection:

Scripture:

Daily Affirmation: I AM...

Be your beautiful YOU!

Date:

What am I grateful for today?

-
-
-

-
-
-

Questions & Reflection:

Scripture:

Daily Affirmation: I AM...

Color, Doodle & Notes

Be your beautiful YOU!

Date:

What am I grateful for today?

-
-
-

-
-
-

Questions & Reflection:

Scripture:

Daily Affirmation: I AM...

Be your beautiful YOU!

Date:

What am I grateful for today?

-
-
-

-
-
-

Questions & Reflection:

Scripture:

Daily Affirmation: I AM...

Be your beautiful YOU!

Date:

What am I grateful for today?

-
-
-

-
-
-

Questions & Reflection:

Scripture:

Daily Affirmation: I AM...

Be your beautiful YOU!

Date:

What am I grateful for today?

-
-
-

-
-
-

Questions & Reflection:

Scripture:

Daily Affirmation: I AM...

Be your beautiful YOU!

Date:

What am I grateful for today?

-
-
-

-
-
-

Questions & Reflection:

Scripture:

Daily Affirmation: I AM...

Be your beautiful YOU!

Date:

What am I grateful for today?

-
-
-

-
-
-

Questions & Reflection:

Scripture:

Daily Affirmation: I AM...

Be your beautiful YOU!

Date:

What am I grateful for today?

-
-
-

-
-
-

Questions & Reflection:

Scripture:

Daily Affirmation: I AM...

Be your beautiful YOU!

Date:

What am I grateful for today?

-
-
-
-
-
-

Questions & Reflection:

Scripture:

Daily Affirmation: I AM...

Be your beautiful YOU!

Date:

What am I grateful for today?

-
-
-

-
-
-

Questions & Reflection:

Scripture:

Daily Affirmation: I AM...

Be your beautiful YOU!

Date:

What am I grateful for today?

-
-
-
-
-
-

Questions & Reflection:

Scripture:

Daily Affirmation: I AM...

Be your beautiful YOU!

Date:

What am I grateful for today?

-
-
-
-
-
-

Questions & Reflection:

Scripture:

Daily Affirmation: I AM...

Be your beautiful YOU!

Date:

What am I grateful for today?

-
-
-

-
-

Questions & Reflection:

Scripture:

Daily Affirmation: I AM...

Be your beautiful YOU!

You
Are
God's
Masterpiece

For we are God's masterpiece. He has created us anew in Christ Jesus, so we can do the good things he planned for us long ago.

Ephesians 2:10 (NLT)

How does it make you feel to know this?

Date:

-
-
-

-
-
-

Questions & Reflection:

Scripture:

Daily Affirmation: I AM...

Be your beautiful YOU!

Date:

What am I grateful for today?

-
-
-

-
-
-

Questions & Reflection:

Scripture:

Daily Affirmation: I AM…

Be your beautiful YOU!

Date:

-
-
-

-
-
-

Questions & Reflection:

Scripture:

Daily Affirmation: I AM...

Be your beautiful YOU!

Date:

-
-
-

-
-
-

Questions & Reflection:

Scripture:

Daily Affirmation: I AM...

Be your beautiful YOU!

Date:

What am I grateful for today?

-
-
-

-
-
-

Questions & Reflection:

Scripture:

Daily Affirmation: I AM...

Be your beautiful YOU!

Date:

-
-
-

-
-
-

Questions & Reflection:

Scripture:

Daily Affirmation: I AM...

Be your beautiful YOU!

Date:

What am I grateful for today?

-
-
-

-
-
-

Questions & Reflection:

Scripture:

Daily Affirmation: I AM…

Be your beautiful YOU!

Date:

What am I grateful for today?

-
-
-

-
-
-

Questions & Reflection:

Scripture:

Daily Affirmation: I AM...

Be your beautiful YOU!

Date:

What am I grateful for today?

-
-
-

-
-
-

Questions & Reflection:

Scripture:

Daily Affirmation: I AM...

Be your beautiful YOU!

Date:

What am I grateful for today?

-
-
-

-
-
-

Questions & Reflection:

Scripture:

Daily Affirmation: I AM...

Be your beautiful YOU!

Date:

What am I grateful for today?

-
-
-

-
-
-

Questions & Reflection:

Scripture:

Daily Affirmation: I AM...

Be your beautiful YOU!

Date:

What am I grateful for today?

-
-
-

-
-
-

Questions & Reflection:

Scripture:

Daily Affirmation: I AM...

Be your beautiful YOU!

Date:

What am I grateful for today?

-
-
-

-
-
-

Questions & Reflection:

Scripture:

Daily Affirmation: I AM...

Be your beautiful YOU!

Date:

What am I grateful for today?

-
-
-

-
-

Questions & Reflection:

Scripture:

Daily Affirmation: I AM...

Be your beautiful YOU!

You
Are
Beautiful

You are altogether beautiful, my darling;
there is no flaw in you.

Song of Songs 4:7 (ESV)

How does it make you feel to know this?

Date:

What am I grateful for today?

-
-
-

-
-
-

Questions & Reflection:

Scripture:

Daily Affirmation: I AM...

Be your beautiful YOU!

Date:

What am I grateful for today?

-
-
-

-
-
-

Questions & Reflection:

Scripture:

Daily Affirmation: I AM...

Be your beautiful YOU!

Date:

What am I grateful for today?

-
-
-

-
-
-

Questions & Reflection:

Scripture:

Daily Affirmation: I AM...

Be your beautiful YOU!

Date:

What am I grateful for today?

-
-
-

-
-
-

Questions & Reflection:

Scripture:

Daily Affirmation: I AM...

Be your beautiful YOU!

Date:

What am I grateful for today?

-
-
-

-
-
-

Questions & Reflection:

Scripture:

Daily Affirmation: I AM...

Be your beautiful YOU!

Date:

What am I grateful for today?

-
-
-

-
-
-

Questions & Reflection:

Scripture:

Daily Affirmation: I AM...

Be your beautiful YOU!

Date:

What am I grateful for today?

-
-
-

-
-
-

Questions & Reflection:

Scripture:

Daily Affirmation: I AM...

Be your beautiful YOU!

Date:

What am I grateful for today?

-
-
-

-
-
-

Questions & Reflection:

Scripture:

Daily Affirmation: I AM...

Be your beautiful YOU!

Date:

What am I grateful for today?

-
-
-

-
-

Questions & Reflection:

Scripture:

Daily Affirmation: I AM...

Be your beautiful YOU!

Date:

What am I grateful for today?

-
-
-

-
-
-

Questions & Reflection:

Scripture:

Daily Affirmation: I AM...

Be your beautiful YOU!

Date:

What am I grateful for today?

-
-
-

-
-
-

Questions & Reflection:

Scripture:

Daily Affirmation: I AM...

Be your beautiful YOU!

Date:

What am I grateful for today?

-
-
-

-
-
-

Questions & Reflection:

Scripture:

Daily Affirmation: I AM...

Be your beautiful YOU!

Date:

What am I grateful for today?

-
-
-

-
-
-

Questions & Reflection:

Scripture:

Daily Affirmation: I AM...

Be your beautiful YOU!

Date:

What am I grateful for today?

-
-
-
-
-
-

Questions & Reflection:

Scripture:

Daily Affirmation: I AM...

Be your beautiful YOU!

You
Are
Very Good

God saw all that he had made,
and it was very good.

Genesis 1:31 (NIV)

How does it make you feel to know this?

Date:

What am I grateful for today?

-
-
-

-
-
-

Questions & Reflection:

Scripture:

Daily Affirmation: I AM...

Be your beautiful YOU!

Date:

What am I grateful for today?

-
-
-

-
-
-

Questions & Reflection:

Scripture:

Daily Affirmation: I AM…

Be your beautiful YOU!

Date:

What am I grateful for today?

-
-
-
-
-
-

Questions & Reflection:

Scripture:

Daily Affirmation: I AM...

Be your beautiful YOU!

Date:

What am I grateful for today?

-
-
-
-
-
-

Questions & Reflection:

Scripture:

Daily Affirmation: I AM...

Be your beautiful YOU!

Date:

What am I grateful for today?

-
-

-
-

-
-

Questions & Reflection:

Scripture:

Daily Affirmation: I AM...

Be your beautiful YOU!

Date:

What am I grateful for today?

-
-
-

-
-
-

Questions & Reflection:

Scripture:

Daily Affirmation: I AM...

Date:

What am I grateful for today?

-
-
-

-
-
-

Questions & Reflection:

Scripture:

Daily Affirmation: I AM...

Be your beautiful YOU!

Date:

What am I grateful for today?

-
-
-

-
-
-

Questions & Reflection:

Scripture:

Daily Affirmation: I AM...

Be your beautiful YOU!

Date:

What am I grateful for today?

-
-
-

-
-
-

Questions & Reflection:

Scripture:

Daily Affirmation: I AM...

Be your beautiful YOU!

Date:

-
-
-

-
-
-

Questions & Reflection:

Scripture:

Daily Affirmation: I AM...

Be your beautiful YOU!

Date:

What am I grateful for today?

-
-
-

-
-
-

Questions & Reflection:

Scripture:

Daily Affirmation: I AM...

Be your beautiful YOU!

Date:

What am I grateful for today?

-
-
-

-
-
-

Questions & Reflection:

Scripture:

Daily Affirmation: I AM...

Be your beautiful YOU!

Date:

What am I grateful for today?

-
-
-

-
-
-

Questions & Reflection:

Scripture:

Daily Affirmation: I AM...

Be your beautiful YOU!

Date:

What am I grateful for today?

-
-
-

-
-
-

Questions & Reflection:

Scripture:

Daily Affirmation: I AM...

Be your beautiful YOU!

You
Are
Chosen

You did not choose me, but I chose you and appointed you so that you might go and bear fruit—fruit that will last—and so that whatever you ask in my name the Father will give you.

John 15:16 (NIV)

How does it make you feel to know this?

Date:

What am I grateful for today?

-
-
-

-
-
-

Questions & Reflection:

Scripture:

Daily Affirmation: I AM...

Be your beautiful YOU!

Date:

What am I grateful for today?

-
-
-

-
-
-

Questions & Reflection:

Scripture:

Daily Affirmation: I AM...

Be your beautiful YOU!

Date:

What am I grateful for today?

-
-
-

-
-
-

Questions & Reflection:

Scripture:

Daily Affirmation: I AM...

Be your beautiful YOU!

Date:

What am I grateful for today?

-
-
-

-
-
-

Questions & Reflection:

Scripture:

Daily Affirmation: I AM...

Color, Doodle & Notes

Be your beautiful YOU!

Date:

What am I grateful for today?

-
-
-

-
-
-

Questions & Reflection:

Scripture:

Daily Affirmation: I AM...

Be your beautiful YOU!

Date:

What am I grateful for today?

-
-
-
-
-
-

Questions & Reflection:

Scripture:

Daily Affirmation: I AM...

Be your beautiful YOU!

Date:

What am I grateful for today?

-
-
-

-
-
-

Questions & Reflection:

Scripture:

Daily Affirmation: I AM...

Be your beautiful YOU!

Date:

What am I grateful for today?

-
-
-

-
-
-

Questions & Reflection:

Scripture:

Daily Affirmation: I AM...

Be your beautiful YOU!

Date:

What am I grateful for today?

-
-
-

-
-

Questions & Reflection:

Scripture:

Daily Affirmation: I AM...

Be your beautiful YOU!

Date:

What am I grateful for today?

-
-
-

-
-
-

Questions & Reflection:

Scripture:

Daily Affirmation: I AM...

Be your beautiful YOU!

Date:

What am I grateful for today?

-
-
-

-
-
-

Questions & Reflection:

Scripture:

Daily Affirmation: I AM...

Be your beautiful YOU!

Date:

What am I grateful for today?

-
-
-

-
-
-

Questions & Reflection:

Scripture:

Daily Affirmation: I AM...

Be your beautiful YOU!

Date:

-
-
-

-
-
-

Questions & Reflection:

Scripture:

Daily Affirmation: I AM...

Be your beautiful YOU!

Date:

What am I grateful for today?

-
-
-

-
-
-

Questions & Reflection:

Scripture:

Daily Affirmation: I AM...